Near
and Far

Ming Tan

Illustrations by
Ali Shandi Ramadan

 **Marshall Cavendish**
Children

Published by Marshall Cavendish Children
An imprint of Marshall Cavendish International

A member of the
Times Publishing Group

Other Marshall Cavendish Offices:
Marshall Cavendish Corporation, 800 Westchester Ave, Suite N-641, Rye Brook, NY 10573, USA • Marshall Cavendish International (Thailand) Co Ltd, 253 Asoke, 16th Floor, Sukhumvit 21 Road, Klongtoey Nua, Wattana, Bangkok 10110, Thailand • Marshall Cavendish (Malaysia) Sdn Bhd, Times Subang, Lot 46, Subang Hi-Tech Industrial Park, Batu Tiga, 40000 Shah Alam, Selangor Darul Ehsan, Malaysia

Marshall Cavendish is a registered trademark of Times Publishing Limited

National Library Board, Singapore Cataloguing in Publication Data

Name(s): Tan, Ming. | Ali Shandi Ramadan, illustrator.
Title: Near and far / Ming Tan ; illustrations by Ali Shandi Ramadan.
Description: Singapore : Marshall Cavendish Children, [2020]
Identifier(s): OCN 1164596240 | ISBN 978-981-48-9391-6 (hardback)
Subject(s): LCSH: Social behavior in animals--Juvenile literature. | Animal communication--Juvenile literature. | Social distance--Juvenile literature.
Classification: DDC 591.5--dc23

Printed in Singapore

For my two monkeys,
one pig, and one very wise rat

Hello!

I like to hug,

I like to touch,

I like to cuddle ...
Sometimes, I am told, a little too much.

They tell me to keep my distance
When we are out on the street,

And especially at the store,
With whomever I meet.

But ... dogs sniff each other's bottoms,

Dogs are very social. Sniffing is a dog's way of discovering the world. Through smell, they recognise other dogs they have met before.

Horses nuzzle to say hello;

Horses use their lips to explore the world.
They show they care by gently blowing
into each other's nostrils!

Chimps pick stuff off one another,

Chimps regularly groom each other, picking off insects, dirt, leaves, and dried skin. Did someone help you bathe or brush your hair today?

And meerkats share their burrow.

Families of meerkats live together in "mobs",
sharing underground burrows made up of tunnels
and rooms. When out looking for food,
one meerkat always keeps watch for danger.

It's not quite me to be alone
So what can I do instead?

I want to play with all my friends
Till it's time to go to bed.

Am I to be a great white shark
Lurking to catch my prey?

Great white sharks travel alone, or in
very small groups. They travel long distances
from coast to deep ocean.

Or a panda in my
bamboo grove,

Pandas spend most of their day eating alone,
their powerful teeth and jaws crunching through
bamboo. They are good climbers and will scale
a tree to get away from danger.

A sloth hanging all day?

Sloths are solitary animals, hanging upside down from trees and vines high above the forest floor. They do not have much time to feel lonely, as they spend most of their day asleep.

It's no fun doing things alone,
Fun is doubled when it's shared.

I have tried talking to my toys instead,
But they just sat and stared.

Well ... dolphins talk by whistling,

Through whistles, clicks, squeaks and
other sounds, pods of dolphins tell one another
when they have found food or need help. Sometimes,
they communicate just to stay in touch.
Each dolphin has its own whistle, like its own name.

Hornbills know their song;

Hornbills are loud! Their big bills and colourful casques (the horn) produce distinctive squawks that their mates can recognise. Pairs sing in "duets", helping them find each other in the thick rainforest.

Bees waggle when they find nectar
So everyone can come along.

Bees work together to find food for
the whole hive. When a worker bee finds
nectar, it will do a "waggle dance"
to let others know where to
find the flowers.

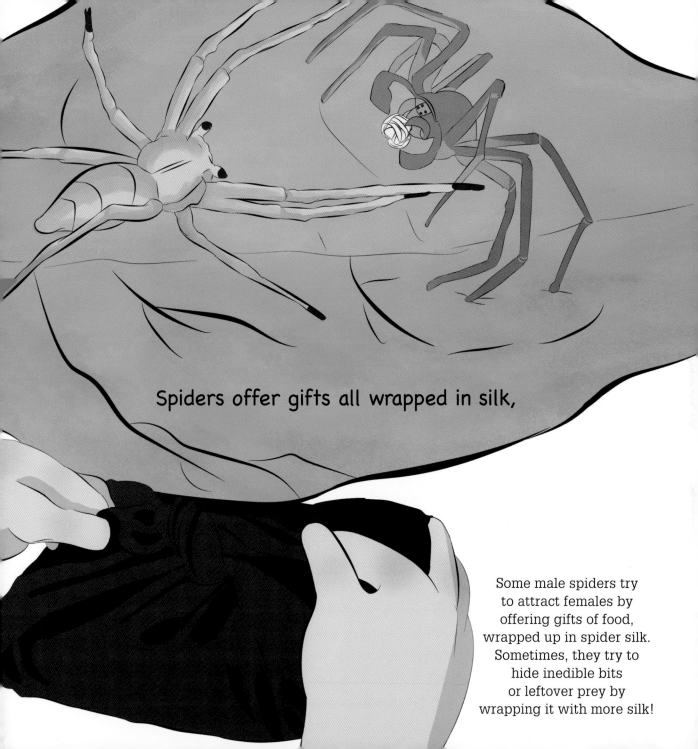

Spiders offer gifts all wrapped in silk,

Some male spiders try
to attract females by
offering gifts of food,
wrapped up in spider silk.
Sometimes, they try to
hide inedible bits
or leftover prey by
wrapping it with more silk!

Elephants rumble across the plain.

Elephants communicate with other elephants in
so many ways – snorting, trumpeting, grunting,
stomping. To talk to others far away, they make
low rumbles that the receiving elephant "hears"
with its feet as underground vibrations!

Lobsters do shoot pee at each other,
But they do not have much of a brain.

A lobster does not have one brain but several nerve centres along its body. It has a bladder in its head, shooting urine from under its eyes when it meets other lobsters.

Even trees know their friends are there,
Through their network in the ground;

Trees are connected underground by
threads of fungi, sending chemicals, nutrients
and water to one another. In a forest, they may
compete, but they also cooperate.

Our friends are all around.

10 ideas to stay connected:

1

Sing out the window (or whistle, like the dolphins).

2

Record a song and send it to a friend (like the hornbills).

3

Do a dance for someone you love (like the bees).

4

Make postcards and send them to your buddies (like spiders).

5

Telephone one friend every day (like the elephants).

6
Write a note on a paper plane and fly it into your friend's house.

8
If you can see your friend's window from your house, agree on a time to turn off the lights and signal with flashlights – four quick flashes followed by two quick flashes spells "Hi" in Morse code!

7
Draw a picture of a friend or loved one, and send it by post to him or her.

9
After dinner, light a candle and think of a friend (ask an adult to help).

10
Plant a seed in a little pot for someone special. Care for it and you can give it to him or her when you next meet!

Author's Note

When schools were closed to stem the spread of COVID-19, more than 1.5 billion children and young people around the world were separated from their friends. This story was written in the first weekend after schools and playgrounds were closed in our community, with national guidelines to stay at home.

The sudden loss of physical contact with family and friends was palpable. To make sense of this isolation, my children and I explored how some animals are very social while others prefer a more solitary life. The conversation moved on to the diverse and wonderful ways that animals communicate with one another. We learnt of the ingenious and special ways different animals use to say "hello".

Nature shows us how we can maintain closeness even if we are not physically together. While social distancing, let's get creative about how to be "distantly social"!

About the Author

Ming Tan was born in Singapore
and spent time in England,
California, and New York, before
returning home with an Australian
husband and an American son.
Two Singaporean children later,
they are a global focus
group for her professional
and creative endeavours.
Near and Far is her first
children's picture book.

About the Illustrator

Ali Shandi Ramadan lives in Surabaya, Indonesia. His designs and illustrations are inspired by manga, anime and his two beautiful children. Ali holds a Bachelor of Arts in Visual Design from the Institut Teknologi Sepuluh Nopember, plays football and loves running around randomly in the yard.